For Normalcy

30 Poems for People on the
Aromantic and Asexual Spectrums

Katie Fouks

Book design by Katie Fouks
Purple texture by BarbaraALane on Pixabay
Frame by PhuongLucky on Pixabay
Gold texture by SinnesReich on Pixabay

Published by Katie Fouks
www.katiefouks.com

Table of Contents

Some Definitions

Aromantic / Aromantic Spectrum – A queer identity meaning a person who feels little or no romantic attraction to any gender or experiences romantic attraction and/or romance in a different way than an alloromantic (non-aromantic) person

Asexual / Asexual Spectrum – A queer identity meaning a person who feels little or no sexual attraction to any gender or experiences sexual attraction and/or sex in a different way than an allosexual (non-asexual) person

Aspec – A broad term for a person who identifies as being a part of the aromantic and/or asexual spectrums

Part One:
The Perils of Being Aspec

Normativity

A baby is born, a new life begins
A blank slate, yet already planned
They look between legs and declare: a boy
With no thought this may not be truth
No thought that *he* may truly be *she*
Or they, fae, per, xe, ze, xie, or e
In time, he will have but one partner, one wife
Certainly not no one, not sad and alone
(They do not consider *happy* and *free* and *choice*)
Two decades, give or take, and he'll be back in this
      room
New son in his arms, next in line
Destiny already planned

Misguided

When I was young, I dreamed of my wedding
A white dress, like a princess
A perfect partner to hold my hand
Now I know love is not for me
(And I prefer suits)

In the heat of the moment

In the heat of the moment,
His lips pressed to mine
And mine to his,
His hands on my waist
Touching me, intimate,
I think:
I can do this.
I can let him inside.
I can let him feel good.
And I can feel good.
I can be normal.
We are on the bed,
Him on top of me,
Naked, vulnerable.
He presses close –
And it's too much.
Too close,
Too vulnerable,
Too intimate.
I push him away.
He goes – they don't always go.
Apologies fall from my lips.
I want to be normal.
I want what others have,
To be intimate, close.
But the sex is too much.
Why was I born like this?

Dating While Ace

"I'm asexual."
"That's fake."

"I'm asexual."
"There's something wrong with you."

"I'm asexual."
"That's an excuse."

"I'm asexual."
"I can fix that."

"I'm asexual."
"You've never been with me."

"I'm asexual."
"I bet you're a virgin."

"I'm asexual."
"Just try it once; you'll like it."

"I'm asexual."
"You've just never had a good partner."

"I'm asexual."
"But you'd still have sex with me."

"I'm asexual."
"That doesn't work for me."

"I'm asexual."
"This date is over."

"I'm asexual."
"So am I."

Torn From My Hands

When you're aspec,
You must make your own representation.
Most writers don't create ace or aro characters.
They either don't know these identities exist
Or they assume these characters are boring.
So you improvise, you headcanon,
You grow attached.
Say there's a woman in this book.
She's a background character,
But her identifying trait is "maiden."
She's a grown adult,
(That happens very early in this setting.)
So it's not that she's too young.
She's powerful, ruling without a husband
As few here are allowed to do.
You headcanon her as aroace,
Because she's not in any relationship
And shows no interest throughout the years.
And then she dies –
In the arms of a female "dear companion"
Never previously mentioned.
You try to breathe through disappointment,
Through rage and threatening tears,
Because now you have no recourse.
You can't insist on the headcanon.
They'll only call you lesbophobic.
(And aspecs get enough of being called homophobic.)
It feels like she was torn from your hands
At the very last moment,

After the book assured you she *wasn't* into women,
That this wouldn't happen – then that.
And yet.
And yet.
You could headcanon this "companion" as a QPP
Or even a close platonic friend.
"Dear" does not have to mean romance and sex.
And yet they will still insist you're erasing a canon
          lesbian –
And in the end you are.
You are.
Because she's not aroace,
She's not like you.
You could never be that lucky.

What if I die alone?

What if I die alone?
It's true I don't want a romance
But I don't want to be alone

What if I die alone?
What if my friends all find partners
And leave me behind?

What if I die alone?
What if my parents die
and my siblings all move away?

What if I die alone?
What if no one loves me in any way?
What if no one cares when I'm gone?
What if no one even notices?

What if I die alone?

The Danger

Every time I mention her, I feel the danger.
If I say "partner," they will assume I mean "girlfriend."
They might be one of the bad ones, treat me badly
    because of it.
And if they listen to my explanation, there will be so
    many questions,
So many terms that need explanations.
Asexual? Aromantic? Queerplatonic?
Every time, I am scared to have that conversation.
I am scared of what they might say, what they might
    ask.
What if they're one of the bad ones?
So, most of the time, I only say "friend."

The Myth of the Perfect Aspec

The perfect aspec is both aro and ace
Fully aromantic and fully asexual
None of this "spectrum" nonsense
They deplore any mention of sex or romance
After all, isn't that the definition?
They remain single for their entire life
Valuing only friendship and family
(They must value friendship and family)
They hate romance and want nothing to do with it
They're afraid of sex and would never watch porn
Or read erotica or talk about it
They're straight, of course – the ideal aspec is
Because they can't possibly be queer, really queer
No attraction is the same as different-gender attraction
It makes perfect sense
The perfect aspec does not consider themselves queer
They certainly don't try to reclaim a slur
And they don't make themselves a part of the
    community
Certainly not loudly, demanding inclusion and respect
    and representation
They do not hog resources meant for real LGBT people
The perfect aspec is silent, complicit in their own
    degradation
Erasure, disrespect, exclusion – *hate*

The perfect aspec does not exist.

Being an Exclusionist

Being an exclusionist is easy:
You gather up every person
Who doesn't fit your definition
Of "proper LGBT person,"
Sweep them under the rug,
Hold them accountable
For "faking it,"
Accuse them of being toxic,
Of pushing your buttons,
For daring to exist.
Did you know *not*
Doing this is even easier?

The "Joke"

I tell you the truth, and you laugh.
"Incapable of attraction!"
You snort, and wine comes from your nose.
You don't apologize as you wipe it away.
"Really! You couldn't just say you don't like me.
You couldn't give the old 'it's not you; it's me.'
No. You're incapable of loving anyone,
So of course it's nothing personal."
Your voice lilts in a mockery of my honest words.
"Or if it's true," you add, eyeing me,
"There's something wrong with you.
Like, you're a psychopath or something.
Or have fucked up hormones.
Have you seen a doctor?"
I don't answer; I don't have to.
Perhaps you'll take my cold stare as more,
More evidence of my "psychopathy," of my "lies"
Of my "it's not you, it's me."
Perhaps you'll leave, and
Perhaps someday you'll learn,
Someday you'll know how much you've hurt me.
Because this isn't a joke.
This is my life.

Fighting Back

You say my identity with a sneer,
A tone of "that isn't real,"
Not a challenge but a statement of fact.
I take it as one anyway;
I hear this too often.
I will not sit quietly.
My fist flies.
Your nose cracks against my knuckles.
Satisfying, bloody.
You cry out, trying to turn away,
But my knee finds your stomach,
Pulling the air from your lungs.
I trip you, and you flail.
More kicks, more punches,
More blood, cries of pain.
I will make you regret what you've said,
What you've thought,
Everything people like you have done to people like
          me.

Only in my head.
You say my identity with a sneer,
A tone of "that isn't real,"
And I turn the other cheek, walk away.
Because I can't show my true feelings.
Your kind would only use my actions against me.

Sad Story

He has the perfect life:
A beautiful wife
Two perfect children
A boy and a girl
A cat and dog
A white picket fence

He doesn't want it
He never wanted it
When he was young
He knew love disgusted him
But they all said
"You'll change your mind."

They meant:
"You'll be normal."
But it never happened
(He knew it wouldn't)
Yet they never stopped insisting
And he could never say no loud enough

(They never knew
And neither did he
The word: aromantic
That he *is* normal
That he is not alone
That he can be happy this way)

So he listened to them
His feelings didn't change
But his actions were what they wanted
What he was supposed to do:
Dating, a wife, a family
No matter how uncomfortable it was

He does love his wife –
Just not the way he's supposed to
He does care
But he can never tell her
He doesn't know if she would listen
What if she didn't?

And now the kids are involved
The guilt is horrible
He hates every day of this
There are good moments, true
But can they ever outweigh
His lie of a life?

So he goes on like that,
Acting, waiting, hoping
That he still may turn out normal, happy
And they go on watching from the outside
Saying his life is perfect

Part Two:
The Perks of Being Aspec

Newsflash

Mom, dad, I have to tell you something
No, I'm not pregnant
No, I'm not gay
Not quite, though you'd understand better if I was
The word is *asexual* and also *aromantic*
Somewhat like the opposite of gay
Or the opposite of straight
I know it's hard to understand
It was hard for me too
But the words make me feel good
Help me understand myself
I am not broken
I am happy
Happier than I've ever been
I know you have questions
Listen to what I say
And we'll both learn

And All the Rest

Most people outside the community are familiar
With the acronym "LGBTQ+"
But do they know what it really stands for?
Lesbian, gay, bisexual, transgender, queer, and
    questioning
Are easy enough, but what is that plus, really?
Let me tell you:
Plus is for those who don't fit so easily into the other
    categories
Plus is for mspecs – pan, omni, ply, and more
Plus is for enbies – genderfluid, agender, genderqueer,
    to name a few
Plus is for intersex – some identify as queer, some don't
Plus is for polyamorous – their relationships don't fit
    the "norm"
Plus is for asexual – ace, demi, gray, and the rest of the
    spectrum
Plus is for aromantic – aro, fray, cupio, and many more
    under the umbrella
Plus is for all these and more, a huge, unique, accepting
    queer family
Remember this next time you see "LGBTQ+"
Lesbians, gays, bisexuals, and transgender people are
    important and wonderful
But they are also just the beginning, just part of who we
    are

Panel of the Aros

Alloromantic: "Aros can't love? They're heartless!"

Arospec: "No, we're not! Some of us still love romantically."

Aromantic: "And those of us who don't still value platonic relationships."

Aplatonic Aro: "Not all of us! Some don't feel platonic attraction either."

Alloromantic: "Everyone feels some kind of love. This can't be healthy."

Aromantic: "Some aros love their pets or hobbies."

Arospec: "Some aros love their homes or ideals."

Loveless Aro: "Some aros love nothing. Some aros don't use the word 'love' at all."

Heartless Aro: "Some aros reclaim and embrace the term 'heartless.'"

Arospec: "All aros are valid, no matter our different experiences and feelings."

Aromantic: "We're united by experiencing romantic attraction and romance itself differently than allos."

Aplatonic Aro: "We defend each other no matter what."

Alloromantic: "No further questions."

Aromantic

Allos will say
Romance is necessary
Only sad people are alone
Maybe they'll never truly understand
A person who prefers life this way
Never desiring that required partner
Truly content with their own company and
Intimacy of other kinds, maybe, but
Certainly not romantic love

Loveless

Love is not a thing I relate to
Only a weapon used against me
Violence against people who are different
Even though my difference hurts no one
Loveless is my defense, my identity
Easy for me – a life without using that word
Some will never understand nor try
Some might relate better than they think

Icon

She is an icon
Spending not a moment on
What people expect of her
She is wild and free – single
"You should settle down."
"Don't you want kids?"
"Do you want to die alone?"
No, no, no
No thoughts are wasted on
Expectations like these
As she travels the world
Chasing her dreams
The occasional night spent
With a sexy somebody
All that she needs
Living her best life

The Risk

You're my best friend.
I don't want to lose you,
But I want something else
(Not something "more"
Friendship is not lesser.)
You've been beside me
Through this whole thing,
From the moment
I started questioning
To the acceptance that
I am aromantic and asexual,
That I don't want a boyfriend
Or a girlfriend or the like.
But I do want a life partner,
Someone to love my way
And who loves me in return,
To share things with,
To laugh and smile,
And cry and cuddle.
It's terrifying to say it, but –
It's you. I want you.
I've imagined my life with you,
My best friend now my
Queerplatonic partner.
The decision is yours, too,
Not just mine,
But I see you're thinking.
I know you understand me.
Please don't leave me.

Even if you say no to this,
Don't stop being my friend.
The silence is killing me – and yet
You're starting to smile?
What is your answer?
Please don't keep me in suspense.

QPPs

I kiss her not
She makes no love to me
Yet we are love
We embrace
We laugh
We cry
We listen
We are love

True Family

My sister a transwoman
Whose birth parents refuse to speak of her.
My brother is an asexual
Who can't keep a girlfriend when she demands more
        than he can give.
My mother is a drag queen
Who will defend any of her children to her own grave.
My father is a nonbinary man
Who need not explain his identity to anyone.
My children are the next generation –
Every queer person,
Every ace, aro, lesbian, gay, bi, pan,
Trans, enby, poly, intersex person,
And all the others.
We are our own family.
When bloodlines fail, choice never will.

Adaptation

My ideal relationship was
Good times with someone I love
Shared interests, shared laughter, shared tears
Holidays, traditions, years passed together
Dates full of romance and, of course, great sex
(Or subpar sex we laugh about
While still having a good time)

Then I met her
Dressed in shades of black and purple
The stripes of a flag I did not know
The word "asexual" was new
I didn't understand
How could she have no interest in sex?
Surely we could never work

But I liked her
She was kind, with pretty bright eyes
And a laugh that put bells to shame
She loved romance – held my hand at movies
Surprised me with flowers and chocolate
Cuddling her while we watched Friday movies
Became the highlight of my week

I don't ask for what she doesn't want
I'm not selfish (though she says it's not selfish to want)
I take care of those needs by myself
Her comfort is treasure in my hands, her safety my
        priority
When we sleep together, it's no euphemism
Only cuddles and a chase kind of love
I don't know what I would do without her now

For Normalcy

Why do I want other people to care?
Huge percentages of people are not ace or aro
And will never know someone who is.
Why, you ask, can't I just be quiet
And live my life the way I want?
I needn't be so loud, so insistent people cater
To what I want or don't.
(It doesn't matter if everyone caters to allosexuals and
         alloromantics.
They're normal; they deserve it!)
I'll tell you.
I want to spread awareness,
Make the world know me.
Make everyone understand,
Know the words, the feelings.
Not assume I'm broken.
Not insist one must have love and sex to be whole,
To be happy, to be normal.
For children growing up to be presented with ace and
         aro as options
Next to to straight and gay and bi and all the others.
To see characters like me in fiction.
To be vindicated to those who would rather see me
         quiet,
Existing in the shadows, if at all.
I want to be *normalized*.
I know that I am normal;
I want others to know too.
I want others to know:

Aspecs are here.
We always have been.
We always will be.
We deserve to be seen and heard.

War Cry

I am loud.
I am angry.
I am unashamed.
I am fighting a war.

I don't blame you for being a civilian
Some are more easily content
Some just want to exist and not to fight
Your life is your own

I am loud.
I am angry.
I am unashamed.
I am fighting a war.

You might say I am joyless
That I won't let anyone else be happy either
I ask you: why should I be quiet, take one for the team?
Why is my happiness disposable?

I am loud.
I am angry.
I am unashamed.
I am fighting a war.

Aces exist. Aros exist. Infinite permutations of us exist.
We are part of this community.
We are part of this world.
We will not be excluded.
We will not be silent.

I will not be silent.

Peace

I am not a warrior.
I am simply a person who wants to live my life.
I don't want to fight or be loud,
Assert my place every time it's casually denied.
I can be happy in my own space,
Even if only on my own.
I value peace.
This doesn't mean I've given up,
That I ignore systematic issues,
Simply that some people are activists, fighters,
And some are not.
I will stand, quiet, strong, for those who are not.

Truth or Dare

"Truth or dare?" Anna asks me,
And Kendra and Lynn exchange an amused look.
She hasn't played with us before.
"Truth," I answer easily.
"How many men have you slept with?
No, wait – how many *people*?"
I chuckle, because the answer is the same:
"None."
"None?"
"She's ace," Kendra explains.
"Sex isn't a thing for her."
"That doesn't seem fair for this game," Anna grouses,
And we all laugh.
Just wait until the next round,
When she asks about my most inappropriate crush
And learns I'm aro too.

Headcanons

Canon aspec characters are rare, it's true
Especially in big fandoms, but we make our own fun
Take my favorite character: a man who's had
Four relationships, all with women
He's also popularly shipped with his male friend
(Less popularly with his other male friend – my
      personal favorite pairing)
But he's so easy to read as aspec in a variety of ways
He could be asexual – we rarely see sex portrayed in
      this franchise at all
And the one time we see this character experiencing
      attraction
On page, he feels great guilt attached – perhaps
      ARCsexual
His first girlfriend died early
The second he wasn't with long enough for much to
      happen
Perhaps demiromantic?
This is supported by how the third relationship went –
Broken off mutually and amiably after they didn't
      really click
Their lives going in different directions, the two of
      them different people
Than when they first met and got together
And that fourth woman, the one he marries and grows
      old with?
He knew her for years before he thought about
      approaching her,

Even longer before his feelings grew serious enough to
        actually do so
And that second friend, my own favorite ship?
They barely spoke for a year after meeting before they
        even became friends
Who's to say his romantic feelings didn't also need that
        time to grow?
And then there's the possibility of a queerplatonic
        relationship
These characters are close, their friendship intimate and
        important
I ship it, yes, but I also love them at their canon platonic
And why not take it in a different direction, put them
        together as QPPs,
Partners in every way?
So he's straight, allosexual, and alloromantic in canon
So fandom might see him as nothing other than alloallo
        gay or bi
So what? In my eyes, he contains multitudes.
He contains experiences people like me share
My headcanons, my way of making characters more
        like me
My may of making characters more interesting,
More than cis, het, allo
Our way of finding ourselves in what we love

The Future is Queer

In the future, everything is rainbows.
Cis, het, and allo are no longer considered norms.
When you meet a person, you always ask:
What are your pronouns?
No one assumes a person is straight.
If you're interested in someone, you ask
If they are interested in people like you.
Everyone knows straight is not the only option,
That person might be gay or lesbian
Or bi, pan, ply, or omni
Or asexual or aromantic, anywhere on those spectrums.
Of course straight people still exist;
Their identity is just as valid.
But it no longer looms like a shadow over everyone,
A cloud, a requirement, a test to pass or fail.

In the future, everything is rainbows.
Anyone can be open in public,
And no one judges your relationship.
Woman and man, woman and woman, woman and
        enby;
Man and man, man and enby, more than two, alone;
Romantic, platonic, queerplatonic, non-partnering.
You can be happy in whatever way you want.
Families rejecting their queer members is rare.
Not unheard of, but if they do,
There is always more family ready to welcome
A wayward, abandoned child.
They are never alone for long.

Queer is family, and we love our own,
Still sometimes more than others,
Even if things are different now.

Queerest of the Queer

I am complex
I contain many things
Many experiences
I am different from most
There are words to explain me:
Transgender, nonbinary, agender
Asexual, demisexual, sex indifferent
Aromantic, grayromantic, cupioromantic
Aroace, angled, queerplatonic, aplspec, queer
Some say these are too many
But each is important to me
Each holds meaning
And some lead to others
Like domain, kingdom, phylum
All interacting and affecting each other
Some say boxes are bad
But I like knowing I am not alone
I am complex
I am many things
And I love them all

Resolution

At the end of my life, being queer won't matter
Any more than any other word used to describe myself
White, woman, aro, ace, daughter, sister, writer, nerd
All of them and more will be parts of who I was

What *will* matter is what I did with them
If one book I wrote introduced a young person to aspec
      identities
If one asexual headcanon made someone see a character
      differently
If one person my mom told "my daughter is aro too"
      felt less alone
If my brother's questioning friend knew our family was
      welcoming

When I am gone, I want to have mattered
If I made life a little easier, just in small ways
For other queer people, other aspecs, others in my
      community
I will have succeeded

About the Author

Katie Fouks is an aromantic asexual writer who strives to represent a variety of aspec characters across a mix of genres. She lives in Wisconsin with an ever-growing collection of nerdy merch and can usually be found obsessing over Star Wars, buying too many books, and pining for her long-distance queerplatonic partner. You can find more information on Katie and her writing at www.katiefouks.com.

Also by Katie Fouks

<u>Queerplatonic Love Story</u>
Ice Castle: A Queerplatonic Love Story

<u>An Aspec for All Seasons</u>
A Queerplatonic New Year
An Aroflux Valentine's Day
Don't Kiss Me, I'm Ace
Greener Grass
We Love Our Queer Children
The Nonlibidoist
Red, White, and Green